EASY TO MAKE

DECOUPAGE

EASY TO MAKE

DECOUPAGE

Hilary More

ANAYA PUBLISHERS LTD LONDON

First published in Great Britain in 1993
by Anaya Publishers Ltd, Strode House,
44–50 Osnaburgh Street, London NW1 3ND

Editor Felicity Jackson
Design by Millions Design
Photographer De Koenigswarter Photography
Illustrators Coral Mula, Kate Simunek

British Library Cataloguing in Publication Data

More, Hilary
Easy to Make Découpage – (Easy to Make Series)
I. Title II. Series
745.54

ISBN 1-85470-180-0

Typeset by Servis Filmsetting Ltd, Manchester, UK
Colour reproduction by Scantrans Pte Ltd, Singapore
Printed and bound in China.
Produced by Mandarin Offset

CONTENTS

Introduction   6

1: HOUSE AND HOME
Enamel jug   10
Vase   12
Tea tray   14
Flowered mirror   16
Waste paper bin   20
Flower pots   22
Storage canisters   24

2: GIFTS
Musical clock   28
Sewing box   30
Glass plate   32
Jewellery box   34
Photograph frame   36
Trinket boxes   38
Hat box   42

3: TABLEWARE
Candlestick and candle   46
Table mats   48
Lamp with shade   50
Stationery rack   52
Ash tray   54

4: CHILDREN'S CHAPTER
Ornamental cat   58
Pencil tub and note box   60
School file   62

5: FESTIVE IDEAS
Easter eggs and egg cups   66
Greetings cards   70
Gift wraps   72
Christmas balls   74
Christmas wreath   76

BETTER TECHNIQUES   81

Acknowledgements   96

Introduction

*Découpage is a French word that literally means to cut up.
However, today this name is given to an attractive craft which
creates decorative objects by adding paper cut outs.*

Découpage became popular during the 18th century, inspired by the elaborate lacquer furniture that was coming to Europe from China and Japan. The Victorians embraced the craft with enthusiasm and it quickly became a fashionable pastime.

The great advantage of découpage is that, unlike other art forms, you do not need to be able to draw to achieve a stunning result. Découpage shapes are carefully cut out and stuck down on another object in an attractive arrangement, then sealed with several coats of hard-wearing varnish.

Nowadays, the craft has been taken one step further with the introduction of all sorts of unusual paint and varnish finishes which emphasize the shapes while adding a new dimension.

About this book

In this book I have attempted to create simple, decorative projects that will appeal to all ages, and can easily be made at home with only a few pieces of equipment. The book is divided into five chapters – House and Home, Gifts, Tableware, Children's Chapter and Festive Ideas – plus a Better Techniques section.

In the House and Home chapter there are ideas for découpage on all sorts of household objects: try decorating a plain wastepaper bin to match the rest of the room's decor, or smarten up a pair of plain metal canisters with cake frills and wallpaper cut outs. There are ornamental jugs and vases, a smart mirror transformed by stencils and 3-D motifs – even plain brown flower pots have not gone unadorned.

In the Gifts chapter you will find a collection of objects that are fun to decorate and a pleasure to receive as a gift. Create dainty little trinket boxes for keepsakes, each one with a special paint technique applied as a base. Make a fun clock from old sheet music, or a stunning glass plate transformed by layers of coloured foil.

The Tableware chapter gives you ideas for practical items such as table mats and ash trays, candlesticks and lamps. There

is even a fun stationery box covered in brightly coloured stickers.

In the Children's Chapter I have turned stamp collecting into a practical pastime and used old stamps to add interest to a small pencil tub and note box. China or wooden animals with distinctive features can be totally covered in flowery papers. Or, you can jazz up plain school files and notebooks with letters cut from sweet wrappers.

Everyone loves making things for Christmas and other special occasions, and the Festive Ideas chapter brings you a whole host of topics to choose from – from fun Easter eggs to Christmas baubles and a holly wreath, each one created out of layers of paper. There are 3-D greetings cards which look like expensive shop-bought creations and gift wraps that guarantee your presents arrive looking too good to open.

Different découpage effects

The basic art of découpage is a simple matter of careful cutting and sticking, but by changing the surface underneath the découpage shapes you can radically alter the whole effect. In this book I show you how to achieve stunningly different results by working over all sorts of unusual backgrounds.

Suitable surfaces

Découpage works well on most surfaces but is traditionally associated with wood. It is the perfect surface for a variety of different finishes, and there is a huge range of paints, stains and coloured varnishes, which can be painted, sponged, spattered or dabbed.

With the specialist paints and varnishes widely available today, wood can also be limed, given a granite effect or aged.

Alternatively, you can leave the work untreated, simply covering it with varnish to seal and give a gloss finish to the untreated areas of wood.

You can also apply découpage to china, plastic, cork or another paper. Before adding stuck-on shapes to a surface, check that it can support the dampening effect of pasted paper and then layers of varnish.

Choose your découpage shapes first, as their style and colour will determine the treatment to use.

Making a start

Before starting any projects, read the Better Techniques section that begins on page 81 as all the methods used are explained in detail.

Basic tools and equipment are described, and you will also find useful information on choosing and handling different types of paper cut outs, as well as advice on sticking and varnishing.

Start collecting paper cut outs, old cards, labels, sweet wrappers, magazines and stickers, to transform objects around your home and create treasured gifts for family and friends.

House and Home

Enamel jug

Smarten up a plain white enamel jug with a coat of metal paint and a handful of quick-to-use floral and butterfly decals – you'll be amazed at the transformation!

Materials
Plain enamel jug
Metal paint (Hammerite)
Floral and butterfly decals
PVA adhesive
Clear gloss varnish
Fine glasspaper

Preparation
1 Give the enamel jug a generous coat of metal paint (Hammerite), being careful to finish the paint neatly round the top of the jug. Leave to dry for several weeks.

Planning the arrangement
2 Cut the decals from the sheets, trimming them as necessary. Lay them out on a flat surface and decide their position on the jug. Using PVA adhesive, stick the decals over the jug in your chosen arrangement. Leave to dry.

After deciding on the spacing, stick the decals on to the jug, using PVA adhesive.

Finishing
3 Give the jug several coats of varnish, leaving it to dry between each one. Lightly sand down the jug with glasspaper between the final coats.

Use several coats of metal paint to cover the enamel jug and leave to dry thoroughly.

Using the jug
The découpaged jug can be used and washed afterwards, but wash and dry it carefully.

Vase

With the clever art of glass découpage, you can turn a plain glass vase into a painted masterpiece, attractive enough to be the centre of attention in any room.

Materials
Plain glass vase, with a top large enough
  for a hand to fit inside
Floral giftwrap paper
Putty adhesive (Blu-tak)
Chinagraph pencil
PVA adhesive
Water-based household or craft paint
  and small natural sponge
Clear varnish (optional)

Preparation
1 Clean the vase both inside and out and dry thoroughly.

Marking the design
2 Choose and carefully cut out the flower heads from the giftwrap paper. To decide on the best arrangement, secure the flower heads inside the vase against the glass with a small piece of putty adhesive (Blu-tak). When you are happy with the arrangement, mark the design on the right side of the glass with the chinagraph pencil. Carefully remove the flower heads from inside the vase.

Fixing the flowers in position
3 Dilute the PVA adhesive with a little water. Coat the front of each flower liberally with the PVA and press their right sides against the glass on the inside of the vase in each marked position. Make sure that you smooth out any air bubbles. Wipe away any excess PVA with a clean damp cloth, to keep the vase clean. Leave to dry.

Painting the vase
4 Before you paint the vase check that all the edges of each flower are stuck firmly to the glass, otherwise the paint will seep under the edges of the paper.

5 Use the sponge and a dabbing motion to apply paint all over the inside of the vase and paper shapes. Leave to dry. When the paint has dried, add a second layer of paint making sure that no patches of glass can be seen. Leave to dry.

6 If wished, the inside of the vase can be given a coat of varnish. Remove all the chinagraph marks from the outside.

Draw round the decal on the right side of the glass, using a chinagraph pencil.

Holding flowers
The completed vase will not stand up to water. If you want the vase to hold fresh flowers, slip another tin or smaller vase inside the decorated vase and use this to hold the flowers.

Tea tray

Brighten up a plain wooden tray with a pretty wallpaper border and a touch of matching paint to make it smart enough for any occasion.

Materials
Plain wooden tray
Masking tape
Matt household or craft paint
Roll of wallpaper border
Soft pencil, ruler, set square and eraser
PVA adhesive
Clear gloss varnish
Fine glasspaper

Preparation
1 Wipe over the tray to remove dust and finger marks. Stick masking tape along the top edge on the inside and outside of the tray. Stick masking tape round the hand holes in the same way.

2 Using a fine artists' paint brush, carefully paint round the top edge of the tray and round the inside of each handle hole. Leave to dry. Add a second coat if necessary. Remove masking tape.

Marking border strips' position
3 Decide on the position of the border on the tray base. Use a soft pencil and ruler to mark out a rectangle in the base of the tray. This will be the position of the border strips.

4 Cut a strip of wallpaper border to fit each side of the rectangle. Carefully cut round the design along the edge of each border strip.

Sticking the strips
5 Coat the back of the first strip with PVA adhesive and stick in position following the marks. Stick on the next strip. Mark across the corner using the set square for a perfect diagonal. Cut along the marked line. Fold back the corner and trim the underneath strip so it is $\frac{1}{4}$in (6mm) longer. Add some more adhesive and smooth over the corner to form the mitre.

6 Repeat, cutting and sticking the remaining strips in position to complete the rectangle. Leave to dry.

Finishing
7 Rub off any pencil marks. Give the whole tray several coats of varnish, leaving it to dry between coats. Lightly sand down between the final coats.

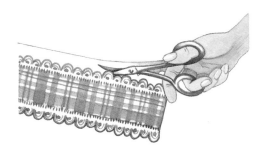

Carefully cut round the printed border, using a pair of manicure scissors if necessary.

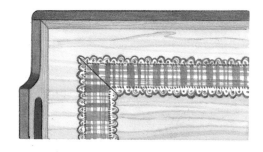

Add more adhesive and smooth over the corner to form the mitre.

Flowered mirror

Transform an old mirror and frame into a flowery masterpiece complete with gold outline.

Materials
Tracing paper
Floral giftwrap paper
White typing paper
Mirror in frame
Spray adhesive and cleaning fluid
Spray gold paint
PVA adhesive
Small self-adhesive stickers
Clear gloss varnish
Fine glasspaper

Making the leaf stencil
1 To make the leaf stencil, trace off one leaf from the floral giftwrap paper. Cut a piece of typing paper the exact size of the mirror inside the frame. Mark 5 leaf motifs round the top right-hand corner of the paper. Cut out each leaf stencil.

2 Using spray adhesive, stick the stencilled paper exactly over the mirror.

Choose a giftwrap paper with a distinctive open flower head design for the large flower.

3 Spray the mirror frame with 2 good coats of gold paint. Leave to dry.

Spray the mirror frame with 2 coats of gold paint, and leave to dry thoroughly.

4 Carefully remove the stencil and clean the adhesive residue off the mirror with cleaning fluid.

Stick flower heads randomly round the outside of the frame and to the stencilled leaves.

Making the floral decoration

5 Cut out small flower heads from the giftwrap paper. Using PVA adhesive, stick flower heads haphazardly round the outside of the frame and to the leaf stencils on the mirror, leaving the bottom left-hand corner free.

6 Roughly cut out 3 large flower heads and 1 large flower head complete with stalk and leaves. Use spray adhesive to stick the flower heads plus the flower head of the flower with leaves on to white paper. Carefully cut out each piece.

7 Use one of the self-adhesive stickers to stick one flower head in the left-hand corner of the mirror. Stick the remaining large flower heads exactly over the first one with a self-adhesive sticker between each one.

Stick on the large flower head, with the outer petals touching the edge of the frame.

Using real leaves
As an alternative to tracing round leaves printed on giftwrap paper, you can collect real leaves from your garden or local park, and use them as the basis for your stencil. Simply proceed as before, but lay the leaves on a piece of white paper before tracing them.

Choose flat, medium-sized or large leaves, according to the size of your mirror, or you can use two or three leaves, of different sizes. Leaves with an interesting outline, such as many of the Japanese maples, are ideal, and can create a delicate, Oriental look. Remember, though, the more intricate the outline, the longer it takes to cut the shape out, and the more patience is needed.

8 Finally stick on the flower head with leaves, so the head is level with the frame edge. Carefully take the stalk and leaves and stick them round the frame with PVA adhesive.

Finishing
9 Carefully paint the frame, stencilled motifs and large flower head with varnish. Leave to dry. Add several more coats of varnish, lightly sanding down the frame between the final coats.

Stick on the flower head with leaves, then stick the stalk and leaves round the frame.

Mirror additions
If you prefer not to use a spray gold paint, the mirror can be treated with Liquid Leaf metallic paint. Draw up the stencil in the same way as before and stick over the mirror. Then use a brush to cover the frame with the gold paint. To use the stencil, pour a little of the paint into a saucer and, using a natural sponge, dab over the stencil to mark it on to the mirror. Leave to dry and repeat. When the second coat is dry, remove the stencil and continue as before.

Waste paper bin

Give your rubbish a floral send off with this decorated waste paper bin. Use an off-cut of wallpaper border and match it up to the decorations in the rest of the bedroom.

Materials
Masking tape
Metal waste paper bin
Pale green spray paint
Wallpaper border
PVA adhesive
Clear gloss varnish
Fine glasspaper

Preparation
1 Use masking tape to mask off the top rim of the bin. Paint the bin pale green with 2 coats of spray paint, leaving it to dry well before adding the second coat.

Decorating the bin
2 Measure round the top and base edges of the bin and cut 2 border strips from the wallpaper border. Using PVA adhesive, carefully stick the strips in place, trimming ends so they butt together.

3 Carefully cut out several large flower motifs from the border strip. Coat with PVA and stick centrally round the bin, overlapping one group with the next, to provide a continuous design.

Stick flower motifs centrally round the bin, overlapping one group with the next.

Varnishing
4 Give the bin several coats of varnish, leaving it to dry between each coat. Lightly sand down the bin with glasspaper between the final coats.

Stick a border strip round the top and base edges, using PVA adhesive.・

Flower pots

Even plain flower pots can be given a new lease of life if they are cleaned up and decorated with a simple palm tree motif. Then they are ready to hold your favourite plants.

Materials

PVA adhesive
Flower pots, about 4in (10cm) high
Tracing paper
Green corrugated paper
Clear gloss varnish

Sealing the pots

1 Dilute some PVA adhesive to the consistency of thin cream and paint over the outside and inside of the flower pots to seal them. Leave the flower pots to dry before decorating them.

Making the motif

2 Trace off the palm tree motif (see below). Mark on to the wrong side of the corrugated paper with the lines of the paper going lengthways up the tree. Mark out 4 trees for each flower pot you want to decorate.

3 Carefully cut out each tree using scissors to cut out the rough outline and then a craft knife to cut round the edges of the trees.

Sticking the trees in place

4 Use full strength PVA to stick each tree in place round the pot, spacing them evenly apart.

Stick the palm trees, evenly spaced apart, to the pot, using full strength PVA adhesive.

Finishing

5 Paint over the whole pot with diluted PVA to create a seal and give the pot a shine. Leave to dry.

6 Paint the pots with a 2 coats of varnish, leaving the pot to dry between each coat.

Trace this simple palm tree motif and transfer it to a piece of corrugated paper.

Storage canisters

Whether they are glass, enamel or tin, storage canisters can be given added sparkle with pretty paper cut outs, making them an attractive addition to your kitchen.

Materials
Storage tins
Cake frill
PVA adhesive
Floral wallpaper
Clear gloss varnish
Fine glasspaper

Making the frill
1 Measure round the widest part of each tin and cut a length of cake frill the same measurement plus 1in (2.5cm). Cut 2 lengths of cake frill, if wished.

2 Coat the frill with PVA adhesive and stick it round the tin, trimming off excess to make a neat join.

Making the flowers
3 Carefully cut out flowers from the floral wallpaper. Coat the backs with PVA and stick them to the tin, overlapping the cake frill or frills. Cut out and stick a motif in the centre of the lid in the same way.

Stick the flower decals on to the tin, overlapping the cake frill or frills.

Varnishing
4 Give the tin several coats of varnish, leaving it to dry between each coat. Lightly sand down with glasspaper between the final coats.

Stick the cake frills round the tin, top and bottom, trimming off excess to make them fit.

TWO

Gifts

Musical clock

To help you keep in time with the music. Old sheets of music are torn into pieces which are then stuck on a cork place mat to create an unusual clock.

Materials
Round cork table mat
Drill and bit to fit clock hands
Spray fixative
4 sheets of music
PVA adhesive
Clear gloss varnish
Clear adhesive
Fine glasspaper
4 red beads and 8 black beads
Clock hands, mechanism and battery

Preparation
1 Drill a hole in the centre of the cork mat large enough to fit in the clock mechanism.

2 Spray fixative over both sides of each sheet of music. Roughly tear the sheets into long strips.

3 Dilute the PVA adhesive with water to the consistency of thin cream and paint over the front of the cork table mat to seal it. Leave to dry.

Sticking on the decoration
4 Using PVA, stick the strips of music to the cork, sticking them in a random fashion, overlapping each one. Continue until the cork is covered, keeping the central hole open.

5 Take the strips over the outer edge to the wrong side of the cork mat and trim to form a $\frac{1}{2}$in (13mm) border all round. Paint over the whole front with diluted PVA and leave to dry.

Varnishing
6 Give the clock several coats of varnish, leaving it to dry between each one. Lightly sand down between the final coats.

Fixing clock mechanism
7 Use clear adhesive to stick the large red beads at the 12, 3, 6 and 9 o'clock positions. Stick the smaller black beads at 5-minute intervals in between the red beads.

8 Fix the clock hands in position in the central hole and insert the battery into the mechanism at the back of the clock.

Stick the strips of sheet music to the cork mat, randomly and slightly overlapping.

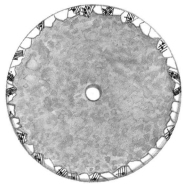

Continue the strips over the edge and trim to form a ½in (1cm) border all the way round.

Timely options

You could use the same technique to get a softer, more feminine effect by substituting strips from two different patterns of floral giftwrap paper, with the same or similar colourways.

For a teenager's room or modern kitchen, use strips torn from bold, geometric giftwrap paper. And for a subtle effect, tear strips of solid-colour art papers, in tints and shades of the same hue: pale, mid- and deep blue, for example, or pinks and reds. You may need to use gold or silver beads and clock hands, to show up against rich or dark colours.

Sewing box

Transform a plain wooden box into a glamorous sewing box by giving it a limed sheen, then decorate with sewing motifs made from button samples cut from a catalogue.

Materials
Large whitewood trinket/sewing box
Wire wool and wire brush
White emulsion paint
White spirit
Liming wax
Clean soft cloth
Button catalogue
PVA adhesive
Clear gloss varnish
Fine glasspaper

Liming the box
1 Rub over the outside of the box with wire wool and the wire brush to raise the grain. Wipe over with a wet cloth to remove any residue.

Use the wire brush to raise the grain on the top and sides of the wooden box.

2 Paint over the box with white emulsion and leave to dry. Wipe over the whole box with white spirit to remove the excess white paint; it will remain in the cracks and grain lines. Leave to dry.

3 Rub over the whole box with liming wax and buff to a faint sheen with a clean soft cloth.

4 Carefully cut out the buttons from the catalogue, choosing ones with a distinctive colour and shape. Arrange the buttons at random over the lid of the box.

Decorating with buttons
5 Dilute the PVA adhesive with a little water, then use it to stick the buttons on to the lid of the box in a haphazard arrangement. Overlap the buttons with each other and mix up the colours and shapes. Smooth over each button to eliminate any air bubbles and to make sure it is well stuck down.

6 Following the same process, stick a few buttons at random on the front of the box, on each side and along the back. Leave to dry.

Paint over the box with white emulsion paint and then leave to dry.

30

Finishing the box
7 Give the box several coats of varnish, leaving it to dry between each one. Lightly sand down with glasspaper between the final coats.

Decorating the inside of the box
To decorate the inside of the box, either paint it or lime the wood in the same way as the outside, or line it with pretty fabric or felt.

31

Glass plate

Wrappers from your favourite sweets provide coloured foil to turn into pretty plate decorations. Cut out old-fashioned 'snowflake' patterns to create the shapes.

Materials
10in (25cm) diameter glass plate
Selection of coloured foil papers
Spray adhesive
Liquid Leaf
Treasure Sealer

Preparation
1 Clean the plate thoroughly to remove any greasy marks.

Cutting 'snowflake' patterns
2 Smooth out the foil sweet papers. Cut each piece into a square, by folding up one edge diagonally until it meets the opposite edge. Trim off the excess. Unfold.

3 Take each square and fold in half, then into quarters and then into eighths. Snip off the centre point. Cut out small V shapes in all the sides of the folded foil. Carefully unfold the 'snowflake' design. Cut as many squares as necessary for covering the plate.

Attaching the patterns
4 Turn the plate over. Spray adhesive on the back of the plate. Overlap smaller squares all round the outer edge.

5 Place the foil motifs over the centre of the back of the plate, overlapping each one until the whole area has been covered. When the entire back of the plate has been covered with foil motifs leave it to dry.

Finishing the plate
6 Use a brush to paint the Liquid Leaf over the back of the plate. Leave to dry and add a second coat if necessary.

7 Trim round the edge of the plate and paint with Liquid Leaf to create a smooth finish. Then coat with a layer of sealer.

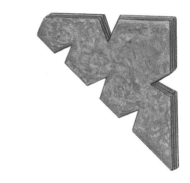

Cut out small V shapes along each edge of the diagonally folded foil sweet paper.

Overlap smaller squares all round the outer edge, then leave to dry thoroughly.

Display ideas
Hang the plate, or a trio of decorated
glass plates, on a plain wall, or use
the plate for serving sweets wrapped
in coloured foil papers similar to the
ones used – ideal for a children's
party or Christmas festivities.

Jewellery box

The perfect gift for friends. They can keep all their favourite jewellery together in one pretty box, which is crackle painted and then covered in stylized fruit.

Materials
Small whitewood trinket box
Yellow emulsion paint
Decal-it
Crackle-it
Artists' oil paint in raw umber
Giftwrap paper with fruit motifs
PVA adhesive
Clear gloss varnish
Fine glasspaper

Preparation
1 Prime the box as necessary, then paint with yellow emulsion paint and leave to dry.

2 Coat the box with a thick coat of Decal-it and leave to dry. Then paint on Crackle-it and leave to dry.

3 When the box is dry, use a clean cloth to rub raw umber paint into the cracks that have appeared on the box. Rub off excess paint.

Decorating
4 Choose the fruit motifs from the giftwrap paper and carefully cut out. Using PVA adhesive, stick the motifs over the box. Leave to dry.

Varnishing
5 Give the box several coats of varnish, leaving the box to dry between each one. Lightly sand down the box between the final coats.

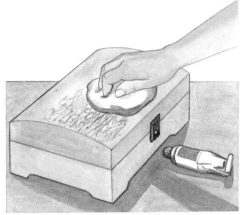

Rub raw umber paint into the cracks that appear in the paint, using a soft cloth.

Stick the fruit motifs over the box, using PVA adhesive, and leave to dry.

Photograph frame

Surround photographs of loved ones in this simple wooden frame, beautifully decorated with bright flower heads stuck one above the other all round the frame.

Materials
Plain wooden photograph frame
PVA adhesive
Sheet of flower decals
Gold paint or gold pen
Clear gloss varnish
Fine glasspaper

Preparation
1 Remove the backing and glass from the frame and leave to one side. Dilute the PVA adhesive with a little water to consistency of thin cream and paint it, using long, even strokes, over the frame to seal the wood.

Attaching the flowers
2 Cut the decals from their mount. Using PVA adhesive, stick the decals on to the frame. Keep the flower heads the right way up on the sides, base and top of the mirror frame.

3 Stick more decals round the sides of the frame and merge the 2 sets together. Leave to dry.

Painting the border
4 Using a sharp craft knife and ruler, carefully trim round the inner edge of the frame, leaving a $\frac{1}{8}$in (3mm) wide border of frame showing. Paint the border gold and leave to dry.

Finishing
5 Give the frame several coats of varnish, leaving it to dry between each one. Lightly sand down between the final coats.

6 Replace the backing and glass in the mirror frame.

Stick the decals on to the frame, keeping the flower heads the right way up.

Carefully trim round the inner edge of the frame, leaving an $\frac{1}{8}$in (3mm) wide border.

Trinket boxes

Trinket boxes are perfect for gifts, and can be used to hold rings and other tiny items. Create different effects with a variety of paint and varnishes, then add cut-out motifs or decals.

ROSE-COVERED BOX
Materials
Rose decals
PVA adhesive
Small whitewood box
Clear gloss varnish
Fine glasspaper

Decorating the box lid
1 Carefully remove the rose decals from their sheets. Using PVA adhesive, stick the roses on to the box lid, overlapping them in an attractive arrangement. Leave to dry.

Stick the rose decals on to the box lid, overlapping them attractively.

Varnishing the box
2 Coat the box in several coats of varnish, leaving it to dry between each coat. Lightly sand down the box between the final coats.

Decals
3 Decals are available in a variety of sizes and shapes, such as the daisy design pictured on the far right.

CRACKLE PAINTED BOX

Materials

Small whitewood box
Blue and white emulsion paints
Gum arabic
Floral giftwrap paper
PVA adhesive
Clear gloss varnish
Fine glasspaper

Preparation

1 Prime the box as necessary and then paint with blue emulsion paint. Leave to dry. When the paint is dry, coat the whole box in gum arabic and leave to dry again.

2 Using a large brush, paint on the white paint, painting across the box and lid in one stroke. Do not go over any section that has already been painted white. Leave the box to dry and cracks will appear.

3 If the cracks look too large, paint over with another coat of gum arabic and then another coat of white emulsion paint. Leave the box to dry between the different coats.

Decorating the box

4 Use a fine brush to paint a narrow band of blue paint round the base and top of the box base.

Paint a narrow band of blue round the base and top of the box base.

5 Carefully cut out floral motifs from the giftwrap paper. Using PVA, stick the motifs on the box lid. Leave to dry.

Varnishing

6 Give the box several coats of varnish, leaving it to dry between each coat. Lightly sand down between the final coats.

FLOWER BOX

Materials

Floral giftwrap paper
PVA adhesive
Tiny whitewood box
Clear gloss varnish
Fine glasspaper

Decorating the box

1 Carefully cut out flower heads from the giftwrap paper.

Stick the flower heads all over the box and lid and leave to dry thoroughly.

2 Using PVA adhesive, stick the flower heads all over the tiny box and lid until it is totally covered. Leave to dry.

Varnishing

3 Give the box several coats of varnish, leaving it to dry between coats. Lightly sand down between the final coats.

SPARKLING BOX
Materials
Tiny whitewood box
Sparkling Sandstones in Dark Jadeite
Floral giftwrap paper
PVA adhesive
Clear gloss varnish

Painting the box
1 Paint the box with 2 coats of Sparkling Sandstones, leaving it to dry completely between the coats.

Decorating the lid
2 Carefully cut out a flower motif from the giftwrap paper. Using PVA adhesive, stick the flower motif on to the lid of the box. Leave to dry.

Varnishing
3 Give the box several coats of varnish, leaving it to dry between coats.

Tips on painting with textured acrylic paint (sparkling sandstones).
● Stir the paint vigorously to mix well before use.
● Paint in 2 layers using a cross-hatch method – paint one way and then in the opposite direction.
● Different colours can be mixed together.
● The brushes can be cleaned in water.

Hat box

An old-fashioned hat box decorated with beautiful flowers and fruit makes the perfect place to store love letters, old photographs (or your favourite hat).

Materials
Flat-packet hat box
Giftwrap paper with flowers and fruit
PVA adhesive
Clear gloss varnish
Fine glasspaper

Preparation
1 Make up the hat box, sticking any sections together for a sturdy construction.

Arranging the decoration
2 Select the motifs from the giftwrap paper. Carefully cut out each flower following the outline. Cut out a selection of fruit in the same way.

3 Arrange a still life on the lid of the box, grouping together flowers and fruit. When you have the result you want stick them in place with PVA adhesive.

Finishing
4 Cut 3 flower or leaf motifs for each side of the box. Using PVA, stick each motif in position, checking that it will not be obscured by the closed lid before you secure it.

5 Give the hat box several coats of varnish, leaving it to dry between coats. Lightly sand down between the final coats of varnish.

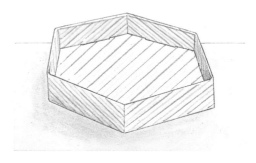

Make up the hat box, sticking the sections together as directed.

Arrange a still life, using the flower and fruit cut-outs, on the box lid.

Design touch
As well as hat boxes, inexpensive, flat-pack boxes come in a variety of shapes, sizes and plain or patterned surfaces – ideal for storing sweaters or out-of-season clothes. Use the fruit and flower shapes, or motifs of your choice, to decorate several different boxes, for a coordinated, 'designer' look.

THREE

Tableware

❧

Candlestick and candle

Dinner by candle-light will be enhanced with an attractive sponged candlestick holding a candle decorated with designs cut from silver and gold doileys.

Materials
Red and silver matt craft paint
Gold stained wooden candlestick
Small natural sponges
Spray fixative
Gold and silver doileys
PVA adhesive
Clear gloss varnish
Red candle to fit the candlestick

Decorating the candlestick
1 Pour a small amount of red paint into a saucer and a small amount of silver paint into another saucer. Dip one sponge into the red paint. Dab the excess on to a sheet of kitchen towel and then dab all over the candlestick. Leave to dry.

Using a natural sponge, dab silver paint all over the candlestick.

2 Then dab all over the candlestick with silver paint in the same way.

3 Repeat steps 1 and 2 once more until the candlestick has a mottled effect. Leave to dry.

4 Spray fixative over the doileys. Carefully cut out motifs from the doileys, reserving some for the candle. Dilute the PVA adhesive with a little water and use to stick the motifs over the candlestick. Leave to dry.

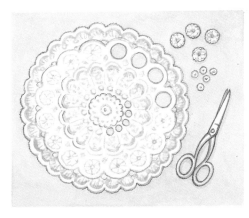

Carefully cut out circular sections from the gold and silver doileys.

5 Give the candlestick several coats of varnish, leaving it to dry between each one.

Decorating the candle
6 Gently heat the back of a teaspoon and press on to the candle. Press the reserved cut-out doiley motifs into the melted wax. Repeat to add motifs all round the candle.

46

Sealing the candle
The candle can be sealed by dipping into hot wax for a few seconds. The candle will be opaque but the decoration will still show clearly.

Safety first
Never leave a candle burning unattended in a room – it's too easy for accidents to happen and a fire to start that way.

Table mats

Clever stamping with an ink stamp and pad can produce brightly-coloured shapes that can be quickly cut out and stuck to plain cork mats to make them look special.

Materials
Cork table mats
Enamel paint
Ink stamp of dragonfly and butterfly
Ink pad for stamp
White cartridge paper
Spray fixative
PVA adhesive
Clear gloss varnish
Fine glasspaper

Preparation
1 Paint the mats with enamel paint. Leave to dry.

Making the decoration
2 Using the ink stamps and pad, mark a series of dragonflies and butterflies on the white paper. Spray with fixative. Carefully cut round each motif.

3 Using PVA adhesive, stick the motifs in place all over the mats in a haphazard arrangement. Leave to dry.

Using PVA adhesive, stick the motifs in place all over the mats in a haphazard arrangement.

Varnishing
4 Cover each mat in several coats of varnish, leaving them to dry between each coat. Lightly sand down between the final coats.

Stamp a series of dragonflies and butterflies on the white paper, using an ink stamp and pad.

Lamp with shade

Give a sophisticated new look to a plain white table lamp and shade by decorating them with smart black and white butterfly motifs cut from photocopies.

Materials

Lampshade and base
Masking tape
Black fabric paint
Photocopies of animal or insect motifs in
  two different sizes from a book or
  magazine (see below)
PVA adhesive
Clear gloss varnish

Preparing the shade

1 Use tape to mask off the top and base bindings round the shade. Carefully paint the top and base bindings with black fabric paint. Leave to dry.

2 If necessary, paint round the bindings again once the first coat has dried. Make sure that the paint is taken inside the frame to provide a good outline. When the paint is dry, peel off the masking tape.

Using black fabric paint, carefully paint the top and base bindings.

Applying the motifs

3 Carefully cut round each of the photocopied motifs.

4 Wipe over the lamp base to make sure it is clean and dry. Using PVA adhesive, stick motifs to the shade. Then stick motifs to the lamp base.

Stick motifs, well spaced out, to the shade and base, using PVA adhesive.

5 Paint over the shade and base with 2 coats of varnish, leaving them to dry between coats.

Note: The varnish may slightly change the colour of the fabric of the shade, as well as slightly rough up the surface of the fabric.

Number of motifs

The number of photocopied motifs you need for decorating your lamp will depend on the size of the lamp and shade you are découpaging and the size of the motifs you are photocopying from a book or magazine.

Stationery rack

Keep all your writing paper, envelopes and letters neatly together in one place in this brightly-painted rack covered in smart stickers of your choice.

Materials
Stationery rack
White spray paint
Yellow enamel paint
Self-adhesive stickers in various designs
    and numbers
Clear gloss varnish
Fine glasspaper

Painting the rack
1 Spray paint the whole rack with white paint and leave to dry. Repeat with a second coat as necessary.

2 Carefully paint the side edges, the base and along the top of each partition with yellow paint. Leave to dry.

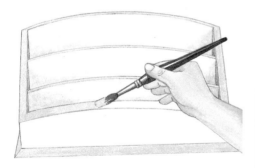

Using yellow paint, paint the side and partition edges and base, then leave to dry.

Sticker themes
There are so many attractive stickers available that you could personalize the stationery rack: fish for a keen fisherman, zodiac signs for an avid astrologer or panda bears for a budding naturalist.

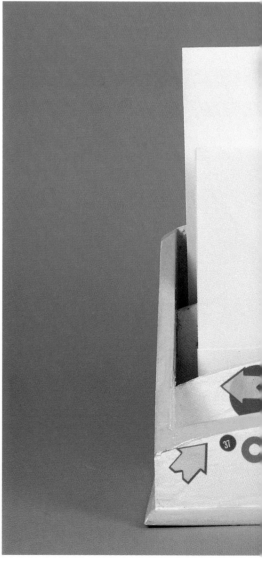

Finishing the rack

3 Peel off the stickers and stick at random over the whole rack, inside and out.

4 Give the rack several coats of varnish, leaving it to dry between each one. Lightly sand down between the final coats.

Stick self-adhesive stickers randomly over the stationary rack, inside and out.

Ash tray

Smart glass ash trays can be ornamental as well as practical. This one is definitely ornamental with its sea shell design made from cut-out giftwrap and sponged paints.

Materials
Sea shell giftwrap paper
PVA adhesive
Small square glass ash tray
Blue and green matt paints
2 natural sponges
Clear gloss varnish

Sticking on the motifs
1 Carefully cut out 5 sea shell shapes from the giftwrap paper. Using PVA adhesive, stick the motifs to the outside of the ash tray, placing one in the centre of the base and one on each of the 4 sides. Leave to dry.

Turn the ash tray upside down and dab with green and then blue paint.

Cut out 5 sea shell motifs and stick one on each side of the ash tray and one in the centre.

Painting the ash tray
2 Stand the ash tray upside down, with the base uppermost. Pour a little green paint into a saucer. Dip the sponge into the paint and dab on to a sheet of kitchen paper to remove the excess paint, then dab paint all over the base of the ash tray. Leave to dry.

3 Pour some blue paint into another saucer. Use a clean sponge to dab paint all over the base of the ash tray in the same way as before. Leave to dry.

4 Repeat steps 2 and 3 as necessary until there is a good mottled effect over the base of the ash tray. Leave to dry before varnishing.

5 Give the ash tray 2 coats of clear gloss varnish, leaving it to dry completely between each coat.

Ornamental cat

Add interest to a plain carved wooden cat with layers of floral paper, transforming it into an attractive and unusual ornament.

Materials
Floral giftwrap paper
Wooden cat with distinctively carved
    features
PVA adhesive
Clear gloss varnish
Fine glasspaper
Small piece of self-adhesive felt

Preparing the decoration
1 Lay out the sheet of giftwrap paper and select the flowers to cut out. Choose small flowers, so they will be able to mould round the cat. Make sure they have a clear outline. Carefully cut out the flowers and leave on one side.

Preparing·the cat
2 Dilute the PVA adhesive with water to the consistency of thin cream. Paint over the whole cat with the PVA adhesive. Leave to dry.

Decorating the cat
3 Coat the back of each flower with PVA adhesive and stick over the cat. Begin on the back and work round the cat on both sides. As you work, carefully mould the cut shapes round the cat's features, making sure that you fit them into each indentation. In this way the cat will still be recognizable when the cover is complete.

4 Keep working over the cat until the whole shape is covered. Take the shapes round the base and over the base edge so there is a border of about $\frac{3}{8}$in (1cm) all round. Paint over with a coat of diluted PVA adhesive and leave to dry.

Coat the back of each flower with PVA adhesive and stick over the cat, starting on the back.

Carefully mould the cut shapes round and into the cat's features.

Finishing the cat

5 Check over the cat to make sure that all the wood is covered and the result looks even and attractive; add extra flower motifs as necessary. Give the cat several coats of varnish, leaving it to dry between each coat. Lightly sand down between the final coats.

Finishing the base

6 Stand the cat on the paper side of the felt and mark round the base. Remove the cat and cut out the shape, cutting ¼in (6mm) inside the marked outline. Peel off the protective paper and press the felt in place over the base, covering the edges of the paper.

Pencil tub and note box

Recycle old stamps by using them to brighten up a dull desk set.
Create a pencil tub and matching note box that will look smart in
any work station.

Materials

Used postage stamps
Blotting or kitchen paper
PVA adhesive
Tub or clean tin suitable for pencils
Note box
Clear gloss varnish
Fine glasspaper
Self-adhesive felt

Preparation

1 If necessary soak the stamps off old envelopes and postcards. Fill a bowl of warm water, drop in the envelopes and leave for a few minutes; the stamps will float off. Leave to dry on blotting or kitchen paper.

2 Dilute the PVA adhesive with water to the consistency of thin cream. Paint a thin layer over the tub, inside and out. Leave to dry.

Decorating the tub

3 Beginning on the outside, use PVA adhesive to stick stamps over the whole of the outside of the tub, pasting the stamps at an angle, each one overlapping the one before. At the top edge, take the stamps over the rim for about ⅜in (1cm). Treat the base edge in the same way. Smooth out all round the tub. Paint with a thin coat of diluted PVA and leave to dry.

Stick used postage stamps over the whole of the outside of the tub, using PVA adhesive.

4 Stick stamps over the inside of the tub but in regular rows, covering the edges of the outside stamps. Coat with diluted PVA as before and leave to dry.

Stick stamps in regular rows over the inside, overlapping the outside stamps.

Finishing the tub

5 Paint the inside and outside of the tub with several coats of varnish, leaving the tub to dry in between each coat. Lightly sand down between the final coats.

6 Stand the tub on the paper side of the felt and mark round it. Cut out ¼in (6mm) inside the marked outline. Peel off the protective coating and stick the felt to the base, covering the edges of the stamps.

Decorating the note box

7 Cover the note box in the same way as the tub. At the corners, snip into the stamps up to the box and tuck in the excess, so each corner will remain sharp. Cut and stick on a felt base in the same way.

School file

Smarten up boring school files and notebooks with simple letters cut out of wrappers from your favourite chocolate and sweet bars.

Materials
White typing paper
Spray adhesive
Paper wrappers from chocolate and sweet
  bars
Stencils of letters in different sizes
PVA adhesive
File and/or notebook
Spray fixative

Making the letters
1 Mark a straight line across the white typing paper. Using spray adhesive, stick the wrappers in a diagonal arrangement across the paper over this line. Alternate the makes and lengths of the wrappers.

3 Carefully cut out each letter using a craft knife and scissors.

Sticking down the letters
4 Use PVA adhesive to stick the letters across the file in a haphazard arrangement. Repeat to stick letters across the notebook.

Stencil letters over the wrappers, using large ones for the file, small for the notebook.

Fixing
5 Give the file and notebook a good coat of spray fixative.

Mark a straight line across the paper, then stick sweet paper wrappers diagonally over it.

2 Mark out stencil letters over the stuck down wrappers. Use large letters for the file and small sized letters for the notebook.

Monograms
Choose initials of names to personalize school files, or use smaller letters and write the name in full. Boys might like their favourite football team emblazoned on their school files, and girls, the latest film or pop star.

——— FIVE ———

Festive Ideas

Easter eggs and egg cups

Bring Easter and a touch of spring to your breakfast table with decorated eggs – real or wooden – and matching egg cups all covered in Easter bunnies!

Materials
Real eggs
White spray paint
Yellow and white matt craft paint
Small natural sponges
Self-adhesive stickers of bunnies and tiny
   flowers
Clear gloss varnish
Wooden egg cups

Blowing the eggs
1 First blow the eggs. Put each egg in an egg cup, hold a large darning needle over the end of the egg and gently tap with a hammer to pierce the shell.

2 Turn the egg over and make another hole in the opposite end. Very gently enlarge the hole in the narrow end of the egg using the needle.

3 Holding the egg over a bowl, blow through the smaller hole until the contents of the egg are forced out of the larger hole. Reserve the egg contents for cooking.

4 Wash out the egg shells and leave in a warm place to dry well before you start to decorate them (see page 68).

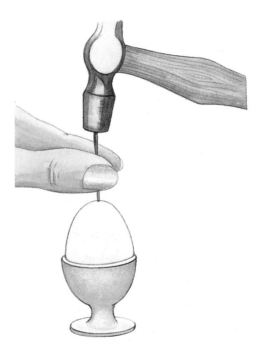

Gently tap the darning needle with a hammer to pierce the shell.

Different eggs
Although chicken's eggs are fine, for a 'larger than life' effect, use ducks' or goose eggs.

If you prefer not to use real eggs, wooden eggs can be purchased from craft shops and then they can be decorated in a similar way.

Eggs in a nest
If you prefer to decorate the eggs alone, and not the egg cups, display the découpaged eggs in a little 'nest' made out of twigs, moss, wild grasses and straw stuck to the inside and outside of an empty yogurt or margarine pot or a small plastic bowl – never take a bird's nest from the wild, since many species return, year after year, to the same nest.

Alternatively, display the eggs in a pretty wicker, moss or lavender basket, on a bed of fresh moss, straw or crumpled green tissue paper.

Painting the eggs

5 Spray paint the egg shells and leave to dry before decorating.

6 Pour a little yellow paint into one saucer and some white paint into another saucer. Dip a sponge into yellow paint, dab off the excess paint on to a kitchen towel then dab the sponge over the shell.

7 Repeat the process using another sponge and white paint until you have a mottled effect. Leave to dry.

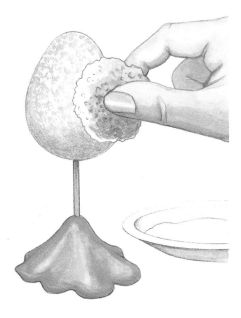

Using a natural sponge, dab yellow paint evenly over the shell.

Tip
● When painting and varnishing eggs hold them on a cocktail stick held in Plasticine or florists' foam block.
● If you prefer not to use real eggs, wooden eggs can be purchased from craft shops and decorated in a similar way.

Adding the decorations

8 Carefully cut round the tiny bunny and flower motifs. Peel off the protective backings and press over the eggs.

Press the tiny bunny and flower motifs over the eggs, then varnish.

9 Give the eggs several coats of varnish, leaving them to dry between each coat.

The egg cups

1 Sponge over each egg cup with yellow and white paint in the same way as for the eggs. Leave to dry.

2 Add Easter motifs in the same way as before.

3 Give the egg cup several coats of varnish, leaving it to dry between coats.

Greetings cards

Whatever the greeting – birthday, anniversary, a special thank you – a hand-made card will show you really care, especially when the motif has a raised 3-D effect.

Materials
Card mounts
Masking tape and rough paper
Matt paint
Giftwrap paper with distinctive motifs
Spray adhesive
White typing paper
Small self-adhesive stickers
Spray fixative

Painting the card
1 Spread open the 3 sections of the card mount. Tape a sheet of rough paper over the 2 outside sections, leaving the front section exposed. Dab a toothbrush in the paint. Hold the brush near the card front and brush over with a finger to spatter the paint over the card front. Leave to dry, then remove masking paper.

Arranging the decoration
2 Choose the main motif for the card, then cut a piece of giftwrap paper to fit behind the card front so the main motif will be centred behind the opening. Using spray adhesive, fix the paper to the card section behind the opening.

3 Fold the front of the card over and stick down to form the card.

Creating the 3-D effect
4 From the giftwrap paper, roughly cut out the central motif three more times. Using spray adhesive, mount the motifs on to plain white paper. Carefully cut out each motif, following the same outline.

5 Place a self-adhesive sticker in the centre of the central motif on the card. Stick one of the cut-out motifs exactly over the first one. Repeat, twice more until all the motifs are mounted one on top of the other.

6 Give the card a coat of spray fixative.

Stick a cut-out motif exactly over the first one and repeat twice more.

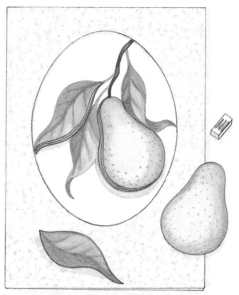

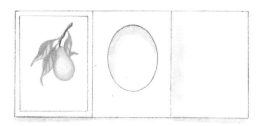

Using spray adhesive, fix the centred motif to the card section behind the opening.

Gift wraps

Cheer up plain brown paper or small carrier bags with clever cut-out shapes and flowers to make the perfect gift wrapping, and make your presents look too good to open!

Materials
Spray adhesive
Doileys
Plain carrier bag
Masking tape
Spray paint
Floral giftwrap paper
PVA adhesive
Spray fixative
Brightly-coloured ready-cut paper shapes
Plain brown wrapping paper
Water-based paints in co-ordinating
   colours

Painting the carrier bag
1 Spray adhesive over the wrong side of
a doiley. Press the doiley over one side of
the carrier bag and mask out the
surrounding areas of the bag.

2 Spray over the doiley with paint. Leave
to dry, then carefully remove the doiley.
Repeat on the other side of the bag.

3 Carefully cut out flowers from the
floral giftwrap. Using PVA adhesive,
stick them in position over the painted
motif.

4 Spray over the whole bag with fixative.

Cut-out shapes on paper
1 Remove the cut-out shapes from their
backing and stick them on to the brown
paper in a random arrangement.

Floral shapes on paper
2 Carefully cut out flowers from the
giftwrap paper. Using spray adhesive,
stick the flowers at random over the
brown paper.

3 Pour a little of the paint into a saucer.
Dip in a toothbrush. Hold the brush over
the paper and rub over the brush head
with a finger or small piece of card, to
splatter the paint over the paper. Fade
out the colour over the background.

4 Spray over the decorated papers with
fixative.

Spray over the doiley with paint, then leave to
dry and remove the doiley.

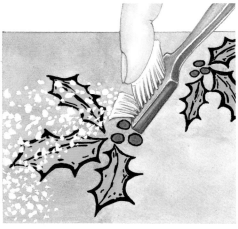

Using a finger or small card, rub over the
toothbrush to splatter paint over the paper.

Christmas bags
At Christmas time decorate carrier
bags with holly and berries.

73

Christmas balls

Hang a few brightly-coloured balls on the tree this Christmas, each one decorated with cheery Christmas motifs, cut from sheets of giftwrap paper.

Materials
Cotton balls, 2in (5cm) in diameter
Red, green and mauve matt craft paint
Christmas giftwrap paper with small
    motifs
PVA adhesive
Glitter glue pens
Clear gloss varnish
Gold, red and green cord and small
    coloured wooden beads for hanging
Clear adhesive

Painting the balls
1 Paint the cotton balls in different colours and leave to dry.

Adding the motifs
2 Carefully cut out the motifs from the giftwrap paper. Divide up the motifs so there are different ones on each ball.

3 Dilute the PVA with a little water, then use it to stick the motifs round each ball. Carefully smooth the motifs round the ball, eliminating any air bubbles. Leave to dry.

Use glitter pens to decorate the motifs, then leave to dry thoroughly.

Finishing

4 Use the glitter glue pens to decorate the motifs. Leave to dry.

5 Give each ball several coats of varnish, leaving them to dry between each coat.

Threading on to cords

6 Using a long needle, thread 16in (40cm) of cord through the centre of each ball. Thread through a bead and form a loop. Knot the cord above the bead. At the base, thread on a second bead and knot cord ends together to hold. Seal knot with a blob of clear adhesive.

Tip
Hold the balls on cocktail sticks held in Plasticine or florists' foam block while painting and varnishing.

Christmas wreath

Use dramatic 3-D découpage to create an attractive and unusual Christmas wreath from shiny red paper decorated with holly print giftwrap paper.

Materials

Foam card
Large dinner plate or pair of compasses
Shiny red giftwrap paper
Spray adhesive
Holly giftwrap paper
White typing paper
Small self-adhesive stickers
Spray fixative
Small self-adhesive plate hanger

Making the wreath base

1 To form the wreath base, mark a 12in (30cm) diameter circle on to the foam card. Either draw round a large dinner plate or use a pair of compasses. Mark another circle 2in (5cm) smaller inside the outer circle.

2 Cut out the marked wreath using a sharp craft knife. To do this, go round the outer circle scoring into the card along the marked outline. Then go round the marked outline again in the scored line this time cutting through the card. Repeat, to cut round the inner circle. Discard the centre.

3 Spray adhesive over one side of the card wreath, then place it on the wrong side of the shiny red paper. Trim down the paper to within 1in (2.5cm) of the outer edge. Snip into the paper to within $\frac{3}{8}$in (1cm) of the card. Pull the paper over the card edge and stick in place on the wrong side.

4 Trim round the inner ring to within 1in (2.5cm) of the inner card edge. Snip into paper at regular intervals to within $\frac{3}{8}$in (1cm) of card edge. Take the paper over the edge of the card and stick to the wrong side.

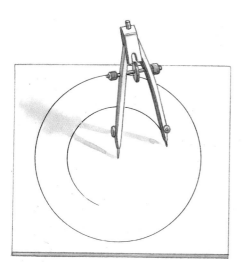

Mark another concentric circle, 2in (5cm) smaller, inside the outer circle.

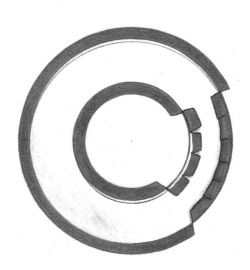

Snip the paper, take it over the edge of the card and stick to the wrong side.

77

5 To cover the base, stand the covered ring on the wrong side of another piece of shiny red paper and mark round the outer and inner edges. Cut out ⅛in (3mm) inside the marked lines. Stick to the wrong side of card ring, covering the raw edges.

Decorating the wreath
6 Roughly cut out bunches of holly leaves and berries from the giftwrap paper, making sure that you have 3 copies of each group.

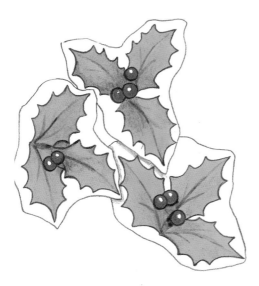

Cut out sprigs of holly leaves and berries, making sure that you have 3 of each group.

7 Using spray adhesive, stick the holly groups on to white paper. Carefully cut out using manicure scissors.

8 Arrange 1 set of each group round the shiny red ring. When the arrangement looks right, fix the arrangement in place by sticking each group to the ring with a self-adhesive sticker placed in the centre of the back of the holly group.

Stick a third group of holly leaves round the wreath exactly over the previous set.

9 Stick the second set of holly groups round the ring exactly matching the edges of the previous groups, but placing 2 self-adhesive stickers behind each group.

10 Stick the third group of holly leaves round the wreath over the previous set, exactly matching the outer edges and using 2 self-adhesive stickers between the 2 layers.

The right spot
Although this wreath, even with its 2 coats of fixative, is too delicate to be fully exposed to the weather, it would look lovely on the front door inside a covered or open porch. Inside, hang it above a mantelpiece, or make two wreaths and hang them either side of a fireplace, sofa or Christmas tree.

Finishing

11 Give the whole wreath 2 coats of gloss spray fixative, allowing it to dry between the coats.

12 Fasten a small plate hanger to the back of the wreath for hanging.

Fasten a small plate hanger to the back of the wreath for hanging.

As well as holly leaves, Christmas wreaths can be made in the same way using flowers or Christmas fruits. However, as you need at least 3 layers of each motif, you may need to buy several sheets of similar wrapping paper.

The self-adhesive stickers can be layered in different proportions to give various heights to the arrangement.

Why not use flower and foliage books for reference. Look at various natural wreaths, find similar flowers and leaves in paper and reproduce these arrangements.

The basic wreath can also be lightly padded to give it a rounded appearance. Insert a thin layer of foam rubber between the covering paper and the card ring. Cut the foam slightly smaller than the card ring, carefully smooth the paper over the edge and stick to the back in the usual way.

Better Techniques

❧

Almost anything can be découpaged as the paper shapes are held in place with adhesive and protected with varnish. In this section you will discover all you need to know about items to découpage, equipment and preparing surfaces for découpage.

ITEMS TO DECOUPAGE

Traditionally, wooden items were used as the base but nowadays many other surfaces are just as suitable. Make sure that whatever you choose is firm and strong enough to cope with the damp adhesive and then layers of varnish.

Cardboard boxes, wooden objects metal containers and glass vases can all be decorated. Each surface will give a

slightly different result: that's the charm of this craft. Begin by decorating a small object, and once you have perfected the art, you can apply it to fitments and furniture all around the home.

Use découpage to recycle old items such as trunks or picture frames.

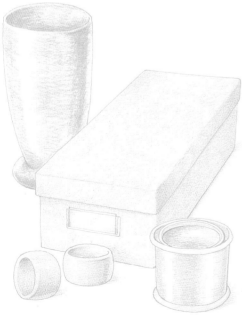

A wide range of wooden, metal, glass and cardboard objects can be used for the base.

Découpage is the perfect way to bring a boring piece of furniture to life or recycle old items such as tin trunks or picture frames. Search second-hand shops and markets for likely items. Before you throw away an old carton and tin, check that you cannot turn it into a useful item again with attractive cut-out shapes.

81

PAPERS TO USE FOR DECOUPAGE

Everywhere you look there are printed papers that can be used for découpage, such as magazines and catalogues, sweet papers and food wrappers, postcards and greeting cards. Use old music sheets or old maps and drawings. Even a photocopy can provide a sharp black and white image.

Use flowers and seed packets to decorate garden objects, and food labels for trays.

papers for découpage are the paper sheets; foil papers are difficult to use.

Decals are bought by the sheet and provide unusual shapes and motifs that are easy to release from their backgrounds. They are useful when you want an old-fashioned look.

You can use images from magazines, catalogues, sweet papers, food wrappers and cards.

Pick a theme that highlights the item you are decorating. Use flowers and seed packets to decorate garden objects, or food labels for trays and canisters for cooks. Alternatively, make an attractive découpage picture of holiday souvenirs.

The two most common souces of découpage material are giftwrap paper and old-fashioned decals, which are reminiscent of the Victorian decals – découpage was a popular craft at that time. Giftwrap paper can be found in many designs, so it's a good source if you want a particular look or motif. The best

Decals are bought by the sheet and provide unusual shapes and motifs.

Thick paper such as greetings cards and cartons can be thinned down to make it easier to use. Soak the back of the whole card with a wet cloth until a layer of paper can be peeled away.

Thin papers can be strengthened (essential for 3-D découpage) by sticking them to plain typing or cartridge paper with spray adhesive.

FIXING THE PATTERNED PAPERS

Spray fixative is available in either a matt or gloss finish. This is a useful way of sealing unstable papers, such as music sheets, doileys or magazine pages before they are used for découpage. Fixative prevents the paper from yellowing and will help seal colours. It will also prevent paper that is printed on both sides, such as magazine pages, from becoming transparent when coated with adhesive.

Spray matt or gloss fixative to seal unstable papers, such as music sheets.

VARNISHES

Découpage is finished with several coats of varnish which seal the surface. In true découpage, coats of varnish should be applied until the edge of the shapes cannot be felt, but on small objects several coats will give the desired effect.

Polyurethane clear wood varnish

This versatile varnish is available in matt, satin or gloss finishes. Matt varnish will give a flat even finish; the satin, a slight sheen, while gloss varnish will give a high shine to the finished article. Choose from either a clear or a tinted varnish, which will change the look of the découpage, giving it a sheen of colour or a wood effect.

Artists' acrylic picture varnish

Similar to polyurethane varnish, this specialist type is more expensive but will not yellow with age. This varnish is also available as a spray.

Poster and watercolour varnish

This is another specialist varnish, which gives a high gloss finish when applied over watercolour paints and papers.

PAINTS

The most common paints used under découpage are household emulsion or artists' acrylic paints, but different paint effects can be applied to a surface before adding the cut-out shapes and it's worth experimenting before deciding.

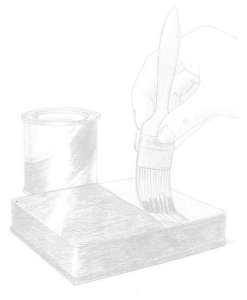

Paint effects are applied to the surface before adding the cut-out shapes.

Household emulsion paint

Emulsion, which is available in a matt or silk finish, is a good base for découpage. Gloss household paint can also be used. Household emulsion does not come in a huge range of bright colours, but you can add colour pigment to white paint to obtain degrees of colour. Pots of craft matt emulsion colours can be bought in a good range of colours.

Artists' acrylic paints

This paint comes in a wide range of colours and is quick drying. Mix it with water to dilute as necessary.

Enamel paint

Small pots of model enamel paint can be used on wood as well as metal to produce a strong, hardwearing finish. It is available in matt as well as gloss finish.

Metal paints

Various paints can be used on metal objects, from car spray paint to specialist metal paints in smooth or rough finishes.

Spray paints

Polyurethane spray paints are a quick way to obtain a tough finish. Some surfaces will need to be sealed with a spray primer before painting it.

If the spray nozzle becomes clogged, remove the nozzle and run a knife blade through the slit in the stem. Then clear the nozzle itself with a pin.

ADHESIVES
PVA adhesive

PVA adhesive is the main adhesive to use with découpage. It is a multi-purpose, easy-to-use adhesive. Thick and white in colour, PVA always dries transparent, leaving a glossy protective surface. It can be used full strength or diluted with a little water to make it easier to apply. To seal items before applying the cut-out shapes, dilute the PVA to the consistency of thin cream and paint all over the surface, then leave to dry. PVA can also be used as a varnish. Once the cut-out shapes have been applied, simply paint all over with a slightly diluted version of PVA and leave to dry.

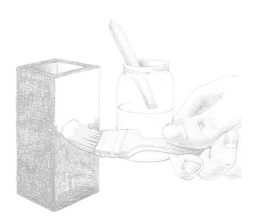

Paint the whole surface with dilute PVA adhesive, then leave to dry.

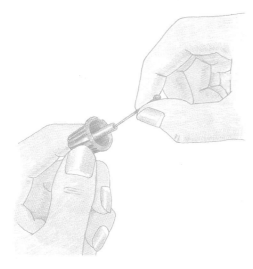

If a nozzle becomes clogged, clear it with the pointed end of a pin.

Wallpaper paste

Similar to PVA, wallpaper paste dries clear and strong. Mix the powder with water to make a thick paste. This paste is very useful as it makes the paper very pliable so it can be moulded round awkward shapes. However, it can also stretch some papers out of shape.

84

Spray adhesive

A useful adhesive when dealing with paper, spray adhesive has a delayed sticking time, which means that sprayed papers can be re-positioned if necessary. Always use this adhesive when working with foil papers on glass (as in glass découpage) as it cannot absorb other adhesives. Use spray adhesive to make thin papers more durable by laminating them to a thicker paper, such as cartridge or typing paper, for 3-D découpage.

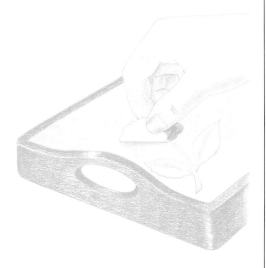

Papers stuck with spray adhesive can be repositioned if necessary.

Spray adhesive can also be used to hold stencils in place while adding the paint.

Always use spray adhesive in a protected space as the fine spray can be far reaching. It is a good idea to make a special spray booth out of an old cardboard carton, as this prevents the adhesive accidentally spraying your other découpage papers or the table top. You can simply put the item inside and spray it quite safely (see right).

Team this adhesive with a cleaning fluid to clear up any residue before varnishing or painting.

Using spray adhesive safely

When spraying small pieces, the spraying can be done with the paper resting on a large area of newspaper. However, it is easy to make a spray booth. Choose a cardboard carton large enough to hold the work for spraying. Rest the carton on its larger side and surround with old newspapers.

Shake the can and spray upright, using a sweeping movement, over the whole shape.

Place the shapes far inside the box. Shake the can and spray upright with a sweeping movement over the whole shape. Handle the sticky work as little as possible when transferring it to the work surface, use tweezers for small pieces. Lay the paper sticky side down over the item and smooth to stick together. Trim round the shape as necessary and smooth over the shape again.

Keep the nozzle of spray adhesive free by wiping clean after use. If the nozzle becomes clogged, wipe over with a cotton bud and cleaner fluid or nail polish remover, then re-pierce the hole with a pin point.

Clear adhesive

Clear, quick drying adhesive is a good multi-purpose glue to use with either card or paper shapes.

Stick adhesive

This type of adhesive comes in a roll-up tube and is easy to control. It is a gentle adhesive that will not damage the paper.

Self-adhesive stickers

Small self-adhesive stickers are used to separate the different layers of paper when creating a 3-D découpage motif.

Temporary adhesive

Putty-like adhesive (Blu-tak) is used to hold the shapes temporarily in place while you decide on the design. It is especially useful in glass découpage when paper shapes are held inside a glass object.

REMOVING ADHESIVES

Adhesive manufacturers will always help with advice about solvents for their products and some do supply this in stores, where the adhesives are sold.

The first step for removing a blob of glue is to scrape off any deposit and then proceed as follows:

Clear adhesive

On skin, wash first then remove any residue with nail varnish remover. On fabric, hold a pad of absorbent rag on the underside and dab on the right side with non-oily nail varnish.

Epoxy adhesive

Lighter fuel or cellulose thinners will remove adhesive from the hands. On fabrics, hold a rag pad under the stain and dab with cellulose thinners on the right side. On synthetic fibre, use lighter fuel.

Adhesive tape residue

White spirit or cellulose thinners may do it. Or try nail varnish remover.

Latex adhesive

Lift off as much as possible before the adhesive hardens. Keep the adhesive soft with cold water and rub with a cloth. Treat any stains with liquid dry cleaner. Scrape off any deposits with a pencil eraser.

Wallpaper paste

Scrape as much paste from the fabric as possible. Spread the fabric over a bowl or dish and pour cold water through the residue. Dab cold water on any remaining stain.

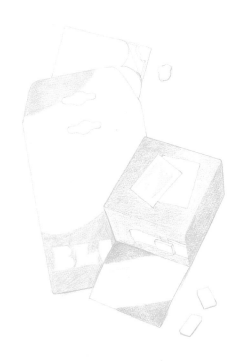

Putty-like adhesive (Blu-tak) and self-adhesive stickers can be used for securing cut-out shapes.

EQUIPMENT
Brushes
Household paint brushes can be used for applying paints and varnishes to items. Use children's craft brushes for applying adhesive and fine artists' brushes for delicate painting. Try to keep the brushes for each medium separate to prevent any discolouring. Clean brushes immediately after use, using water for water-based paints and white spirit for varnish.

Use household paint brushes, children's craft brushes and fine artists' brushes.

Hole punches
Hole punches are a useful addition to découpage equipment as they can be used to create perfect circles of paper or foil.

Glasspaper
Glasspaper is available in a variety of grades from extremely fine to very coarse. Use coarser grades for rubbing down surfaces before painting. If several layers of varnish are used over the découpaged shapes, use a fine glasspaper to gently sand down in between the final coats.

Masking tape
Masking tape can be combined with rough off-cuts of paper to mask off areas when using spray paints.

Scissors
Two main types of scissors are used for découpage. When cutting out the delicate shapes for découpage, use a small pair of

Use curved manicure scissors for cutting round delicate shapes.

curved manicure scissors. Large, sharp-pointed scissors can be used first to isolate a particular motif.

Craft knives
When cutting straight edges, use a craft knife or scalpel against a metal ruler.

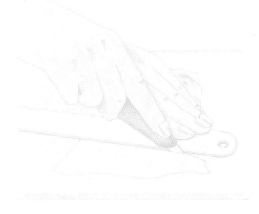

To cut straight edges, use a sharp craft knife or scalpel against a metal ruler.

BASIC TECHNIQUES

As with any art or craft, before you begin check that you have all the materials and equipment that you need. Work with a cutting mat to hand for cutting with a craft knife and cover the surface with rough paper off-cuts or newspaper when using paint and varnish.

Planning a design

The best thing about découpage is that you do not need to be able to draw to achieve a stunning result: the composition of any design is the placement of the cut-out shapes.

Before you begin, decide how you want the finished item to look. This will give you some idea of the type of paper you need to use to achieve this result. Lay the paper out on a flat surface and decide which part of the design you want to use, then cut out the shapes.

Once you have an array of cut-out shapes, arrange them into an attractive design.

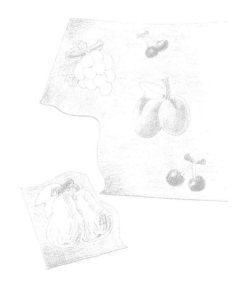

Lay the paper on a flat surface and decide which part of the design you want to use.

The shapes do not need to be cut out individually; for example, groups of flowers can be cut out together. Once you have an array of cut-out shapes on a flat surface, you can arrange them into a design. The item that you are découpaging will help you make the decision when planning the arrangement as it will dictate the amount of surface on which you can place the shapes.

Once you are happy with the design, either draw round the shapes on a plain sheet of paper and use this as a guide when securing the real thing, or use putty adhesive (Blu-tack) to hold the shapes temporarily in position on the object you are decorating and remove it as you stick each shape firmly in place. If you are not confident about your design skills, just cut out as many shapes as you can and simply cover the whole item, arranging the cut-out shapes in straight rows or overlapping them in a random effect.

Fixing the papers

If you are unsure of any of the papers you are using, or the paper is two-sided, spray over the whole sheet on both sides with fixative and leave to dry before you cut out the shapes. This will provide the paper with a protective surface and also stop the paper from turning yellow with age.

Preparing different surfaces

Once the cut-out shapes are in place the item will simply be varnished. If you want a different or unusual paint finish on the item, this must be done before the shapes are stuck down.

Rub the surface of the item to remove any old paint or varnish, or to simply smooth down a new surface. Wipe away the dust with a damp cloth. On glass and ceramic pieces, just make sure that the surfaces are clean and free from grease.

outline. On shapes where the outline is unclear either use a soft pencil to mark in a line to follow or gently curve the cutting line to give an attractive edge to the shape. Hold the scissor blades at a slight angle away from you as you cut round a shape. By cutting the paper at an angle you create a bevelled edge, making the heavy cutting line less obvious.

Use a sharp craft knife or a scalpel and a metal ruler to cut straight edges. Use straight blades and keep changing them as damaged blades will drag the paper rather than cutting it. Always cut on a special cutting mat so as not to ruin the working surface.

Use a set square and ruler to check right angles and parallel lines. Line up the straight metal edge against the line to be cut. Press the craft knife against the metal edge and firmly draw the knife towards you, keeping an even pressure on the straight edge to keep it still.

Using a damp cloth, wipe away any dust on the item to be decorated.

Use a set square and ruler to check right angles and parallel lines.

Cutting out the shapes

Lay out the paper and choose which motifs you want to use. Roughly cut out each motif with large scissors, leaving a good margin all round.

Change to small curved manicure scissors and carefully cut round the

If the paper is thick, score the cutting line gently to mark it, then, still with the straight edge in position, cut along the line again, pressing harder on the craft knife to cut through the paper.

To cut round curves, mark the shape lightly with the knife point and cut round making sure that the free hand is pressing firmly on the paper to keep it still, but out of the way of the knife's path. To cut small shapes with right angles and tight curves, start by piercing the corner point of each shape with the point of the blade and cut away from the corner, drawing the knife towards you. This should ensure neatly cut points.

Alternatively, paper can be torn into strips or small pieces. When you tear a piece of paper along its grain the paper rips easily and the torn edge is fairly even. Paper torn across the grain leaves a jagged edge which can be attractive, but it is more difficult to control the torn edge.

Sticking the shapes in place
Apply a layer of adhesive to the back of the shape (in glass découpage the adhesive is applied to the front) with a paint brush, making sure that the whole shape has been covered. Use tweezers to pick up tiny glued shapes. Lay the shapes over the item and gently smooth in place with your fingers and a damp cloth to eliminate air bubbles and excess adhesive. Once the shapes are in the correct position, check that they are firmly stuck together. If a piece is loose, use a cocktail stick to slip some adhesive under the paper edge.

To cut right angles and tight curves, pierce the paper and draw the knife towards you.

To keep fingers clean, use tweezers to pick up tiny sticky shapes.

To cut curves, use the free hand to press firmly on the paper, but out of the knife's path.

Varnishing
Traditionally, découpage had up to 20 layers of varnish over the cut-out shapes, so the edges of the shapes merged into the background. However with today's varnishes, with good total coverage, only 8–10 coats are now necessary.

When varnishing, make sure that it is applied in a dust free atmosphere as tiny particles can settle on the surface and spoil the effect. Use a household paint brush and work with long even strokes across the item. Do not overload the brush; it is far better to apply several fine layers of varnish rather than a couple of heavy ones which may run and spoil the decorated item.

Use a household paint brush and work with long, even strokes across the item.

Use a fine glasspaper between the final coats. Work gently along the grain and wipe away the dust created. As an alternative, use a good quality wax to finish off the découpaged item.

PAINT FINISHES
A more sophisticated technique is to change the surface of the item with an attractive paint finish before adding the cut-out shapes. The following are the most popular methods:

Sponging
Use natural sponges and emulsion paints. Choose the sponges with care: for small items it should be a small cosmetic sponge which will have a finer mesh. Rinse out the sponge in water before you begin, but make sure that the sponge is not too wet or the paint will run. The item must first have a base coat on which to build the sponging.

Pour the paints to be used into clean saucers so you can dip the sponges in with ease. Keep a few sheets of plain paper or kitchen towel beside you ready for testing the effect. Dip the sponge into the first colour and dab it on to the paper or kitchen towel to remove the excess paint and show you the effect. Then dab the paint all over the item and allow to dry. Dip a new sponge into the second colour and work over the item in the same way; leave to dry. If the colours look too separate, repeat the process until you have a good mottled effect with the colours merging but with some of the background still showing through.

Dip a new sponge into the second colour and work over the item in the same way.

Liming

A pale sheen can be produced on wooden items by liming, and it makes an attractive finish on which to stick cut-out shapes. Liming should be done straight on to new unfinished wood. The grain of the wood must first be raised by rubbing with wire wool or a wire brush: the liming wax then sits in the grain cracks and lines.

Apply the liming wax over the whole surface and rub into the wood.

Apply the liming wax over the whole surface and rub into the wood. Then use a new soft cloth to buff off the wax and give the wood a deep sheen.

If you want a pale colour, give the wood an all-over wash with white or a very pale colour emulsion paint before waxing. Then wipe off the excess paint with white spirit before applying the wax in the same way as before.

Stencilling

Simple motifs can be traced off the decorative papers used for the découpage shapes and turned into a stencil to use together with the cut-out shapes.

Trace off the outline from the paper and mark it on to acetate or stencil card. For one-off designs that will only be used once, the outlines can be cut from a piece of thick paper. You can use just an outline or you can make a more intricate stencil with bridges across the shape to give it more of a pattern.

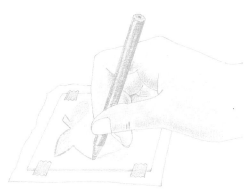

Trace the outline from the paper and mark it on to the acetate or stencil card.

To form continuous patterns, use shapes with linking sides such as leaves.

92

Tape rough paper along the edges on either side of the stencil, using masking tape.

Once you are happy with the design, carefully cut out the stencil using small manicure scissors or a sharp craft knife. Use spray adhesive to hold the stencil firmly in place against the item: this will prevent any paint from seeping underneath the edges. Tape rough paper along the edges on either side of the stencil with masking tape, to protect the rest of the item.

Use paint and a stubby stencil brush and dab over the stencil to cover the cut-out stencil shape with paint. Or use a spray paint and work across the stencil with even movements back and forth. Leave to dry before removing the stencil.

Spatter painting

This is a simple decorative form that leaves the item with specks of paint dotted all over the surface. On small areas, you can use a clean toothbrush to produce an interesting effect. Mask off the outer areas well, as the paint droplets can go over a wide distance when spattering. Use masking tape and rough paper to isolate the area to be decorated.

Pour the paint into a clean saucer. Dip the toothbrush into the saucer then,

Dab over the cut-out stencil shape, using paint and a stubby stencil brush.

Brush your finger backwards and forwards across the toothbrush head, to spatter paint.

holding it in front of the item, brush your finger backwards and forwards across the brush head, so the paint flies off in small specks. As with sponging, 2 or more colours can be speckled one on top of the other, but do let the first colour dry before adding further coats of different colours.

Alternatively, brush 2 small toothbrushes together to create the same effect or rub a small piece of card across the brush top.

Crackle effects

To produce a paint crackle effect, 2 different emulsion paints are layered one on top of the other, with a layer of gum arabic in between. The top layer then cracks open to reveal the one below.

Paint on the first coat of emulsion and leave to dry. Apply a thick layer of gum arabic over the whole item, leave to dry, then paint over with the second emulsion colour, brushing over the surface in one movement. Do not go back over the same area as it will ruin the effect. Cracks will start to appear in the paint and the base paint will be revealed. The gum

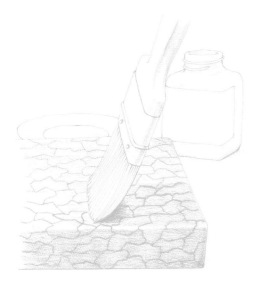

Re-apply gum arabic and the second paint colour over the cracks, for a finer finish.

arabic and second paint colour can be re-applied for a finer finish. After the shapes have been stuck in place varnish over the whole item.

To apply a crackle varnish, 2 varnishes are painted in layers to create the effect as before. The first layer is a coat of oil-based varnish. Leave until it is tacky then apply a coat of water-based varnish or gum arabic and leave to dry. Cracks will start to appear.

To increase the effect, rub an oil-based paint in a dark colour such as raw umber to highlight the cracks. Buff over with a soft clean cloth. Add the cut out shapes and then varnish over the whole item. Crackle varnish kits are also available plus bottles of specialist crackle glaze solutions.

Gilding

As an alternative to metallic paints, gilding is a good way to achieve a gold-effect either as an all-over surface or in small areas. Combine the gilding wax with a ready-made gesso, which gives the surface a good matt finish on which to add the gilt. Paint the surface with gesso first and leave to dry. When dry, apply the gilt wax either with a finger or with a cloth pad. Rub over the surface sparingly and leave some areas untouched so the colour shows through on the surface. This will give a lovely antique effect to the surface.

Buff over with a soft cloth to seal the result and give the whole surface a subtle sheen.

Caring for brushes

Always clean brushes immediately after you have finished using them.
- To wash brushes that were used with water or acrylic paints, hold the brush under the cold tap, to remove excess paint. Then add soap or washing-up liquid and gently rub the bristles in the palm of your hand to achieve a good lather.
- Rinse and repeat, until all the paint is removed. Leave brushes, bristle head uppermost in a jam jar to dry.

- To clean brushes used for oil painting, rinse off the excess paint in white spirit. Then follow the cleaning process for water-based paints and store in the same way (see left).

(see left)

Hints and tips for painting and varnishing

Before you start to paint or varnish, you must bear a few rules in mind.
- Always work in a well-ventilated room.
- Never smoke while painting or varnishing.
- Wear PVC or vinyl gloves to protect your hands.
- Wear overalls or an apron to protect clothes and prevent small particles of lint from sticking to the object.
- Work in a warm, dry atmosphere to aid drying.
- Prepare the surface properly before you begin. Make sure that it is completely dry and free from dust. Check the surrounding area is dust free too. Lay down protective layers of newspaper or brown paper and replace after sanding.
- Always follow the manufacturers' instructions.
- When adding layers of colours such as in sponging, begin with a light colour and add darker shades on top.

Giving a synthetic sponge the natural look

Natural sponges can be quite expensive, but using a synthetic sponge can give you an unexciting repeat print. However, you can transform a synthetic decorators' sponge to give you a more natural effect.

Using small scissors, snip random pieces out of sponge, to create a natural effect.

First, trim off any hard edges forming the sponge into a rounded shape. Then graduate the edges to give a more natural outline. Using sharp-pointed scissors, cut out tiny pieces from the sponge to make the surface uneven. Snip out small and large pieces all over until the whole surface is uneven and more like a natural sponge. Repeat on the other side of the sponge.

Acknowledgements

The author would like to thank the
following for their help.
Bexfield Scissors, Sheffield, S31 8NP.
Button Treasures, London EC1M 7AN.
Decals from Mamelok Press,
Bury St. Edmunds IP32 6NJ.
First Class Stamps, Fakenham, Norfolk
NR21 9BW.
Fred Aldous, Manchester M60 1UX.
Hallmark Cards, Henley-on-Thames,
Oxon RG9 1LQ.
Newey Goodman, Tipton, DY4 8AH.
Sanderson, London W1M 9HA
Swancraft, Canterbury CT1 1DX.
Zweckform UK., Herts SG13 7AY.